Stations of the Cross
with
Our Sister Saint Thérèse

By the Author

Something New with St. Thérèse:
Her Eucharistic Miracle

Being Catholic:
What Every Catholic Should Know

The Paradise Project

Homeschooling with Gentleness

A Little Way of Homeschooling

❧

Edited by the Author

Selected Sermons of
Thomas Aquinas McGovern, S. J.

Stations of the Cross with Our Sister Saint Thérèse

Suzie Andres

Little Way
BOOKS

Copyright © 2020 by Suzie Andres

Printed in the United States of America. All rights reserved.

Cover design by Miriam Schroder

Interior design by Nora Malone

Cover image: Therese as novice in white mantle, Carmel of Lisieux, January 1889 (age 16)

Interior images:
Station images courtesy of CCWatershed.org.

Holy Face of the Carmel of Lisieux (after the Shroud of Turin), 1905, by Céline Martin, Sister Génevieve of the Holy Face and St. Thérèse.

Christ Crucified, by Diego Velázquez, c. 1632, image courtesy of Wikimedia Commons, public domain.

No part of this book may be reproduced, stored in a retrieval system, or transmitted in any form, or by any means, electronic, mechanical, photocopying, or otherwise, without the prior written permission of the publisher, except by a reviewer, who may quote brief passages in a review.

ISBN 978-1-7347093-1-5

First printing

For Paul and Finn

*"Courage! It is I!
Do not be afraid."
(Mt 14:27)*

"The pious exercise of the Way of the Cross represents the sorrowful journey that Jesus Christ made with the cross on His shoulders, to die on Calvary for the love of us. We should, therefore, practice this devotion with the greatest possible fervor, placing ourselves in spirit beside our Savior as He walked this sorrowful way, uniting our tears with His, and offering to Him both our compassion and our gratitude."

—St. Alphonsus de Ligouri

Contents

✤

Opening Prayers 1

Prayer before a Crucifix 33

Act of Oblation to Merciful Love 34

A Note on Indulgences 38

A Note on Special Plenary Indulgences
    in the Time of Coronavirus 41

Guardian Angel Prayer (When Unable
    to Assist at Holy Mass) 46

> *"May your soul, may your heart, may everything about you be filled with candour in your relations with Jesus."*
>
> —Servant of God Marcel Van,
> spiritual little brother of St. Thérèse

Stations of the Cross with Our Sister Saint Thérèse

✤

Opening Prayers

Jesus, adorable even in Your bitter Passion, we desire with Saint Thérèse to love You and make You loved. Send Your Holy Spirit to enlighten our minds and enflame our hearts as we walk with You along this little way of the Cross.

Blessed Mother, you were the first to accompany Your Son, the sweet Spouse of our souls, along the way of the Cross. Wrap us in your mantle and accompany us on this journey today and always.

Guardian angel, you never leave my side. Help me to know and remember the infinitely tender love with which Jesus suffered and died for me. Amen.

I

JESUS IS CONDEMNED TO DEATH

"They shouted all the louder, 'Crucify Him!' So Pilate, anxious to placate the crowd … having ordered Jesus to be scourged, handed Him over to be crucified." (Mk 15:15)

We adore Thee, O Christ, and we bless Thee,
Because by Thy Holy Cross, Thou hast redeemed the world.

From St. Thérèse

"O Jesus! When Thou wast a wayfarer upon earth, Thou didst say, 'Learn of Me, for I am Meek and Humble of Heart, and you shall find rest for your souls.'"

"I've never acted like Pilate, who refused to listen to the truth. I've always said to God: O my God, I really want to listen to You; I beg You to answer me when I say humbly: What is truth? Make me see things as they really are. Let nothing cause me to be deceived."

"It is a great trial to see only the dark side of things.... Do what you can to detach your heart from earthly cares ... then feel certain that Jesus will do the rest."

Our Father ...

II

JESUS CARRIES HIS HEAVY CROSS FOR US

"And when they had mocked Him, they stripped Him of the purple cloak, dressed Him in His own clothes, and led Him out to crucify Him ... and He went out, bearing His own cross." (Mk 15:20; Jn 19:17)

We adore Thee, O Christ, and we bless Thee,
Because by Thy Holy Cross, Thou hast redeemed the world.

From St. Thérèse

"Since Jesus has gone back to Heaven I can follow Him only by the path He has traced. How luminous are His footprints—diffusing a divine sweetness."

"What is our humiliation at the moment is our glory later on, even in this life."

"Yes, Jesus is there with His cross! Privileged one of His love, He wills to make you like Him! Why be frightened at not being able to carry this cross without weakening?"

Hail Mary . . .

III

JESUS FALLS FOR THE FIRST TIME

"I looked around, but there was no one to help ... no one to sustain me." (Is 63:5)

We adore Thee, O Christ, and we bless Thee,
Because by Thy Holy Cross, Thou hast redeemed the world.

From St. Thérèse

"What does it matter, my Jesus, if I fall at each moment; I see my weakness through this and this is a great gain for me."

"Since our Well-Beloved has *trodden the wine press alone* (Is 63:3)—the wine which He gives us to drink—in our turn let us not refuse to wear garments dyed with blood, let us press out for Jesus a new wine which may slake His thirst, and *looking around Him* He will no longer be able to say that He is alone; we shall be there *to help*."

"My Beloved, Your example invites me to humble myself, to scorn honors. To delight You I want to stay little. In forgetting myself, I'll charm Your Heart."

Glory Be...

IV

JESUS MEETS HIS AFFLICTED MOTHER

"Simeon blessed them and said to Mary, His Mother, 'This child is destined to be a sign of contradiction, and thy own heart a sword shall pierce.'" (Lk 2:34-35)

We adore Thee, O Christ, and we bless Thee,
Because by Thy Holy Cross, Thou hast redeemed the world.

From St. Thérèse

"During this sorrowful exile, O my beloved Mother, I want to live with you ... then follow you to Heaven someday."

"The Blessed Virgin never fails to protect me as soon as I invoke her. In my troubles and anxieties I very quickly invoke her and, like the most tender of mothers, she always takes care of my interests. Try it, and you'll see."

"Not being able to bear it any longer, I asked the Blessed Virgin to take my head in her hands and support it."

Our Father ...

V

SIMON OF CYRENE HELPS JESUS CARRY HIS CROSS

*"And they compelled a passer-by ...
to carry His cross." (Mk 15:21)*

We adore Thee, O Christ, and we bless Thee,
Because by Thy Holy Cross, Thou hast redeemed the world.

From St. Thérèse

"Jesus gives me at every moment what I am able to bear and nothing more, and if in the next moment He increases my suffering, He also increases my strength."

"If we can say that our sacrifices are like locks of hair that captivate the heart of Christ, we must likewise say that our joys affect Him in a like manner."

"We must serve our Lord; sow what is good around us without worrying about its growth. For us the labors; for Jesus, success!"

Hail Mary...

VI

VERONICA WIPES THE FACE OF JESUS

"He had no form or comeliness that we should look at Him, and no beauty that we should desire Him." (Is 53:2)

We adore Thee, O Christ, and we bless Thee,
Because by Thy Holy Cross, Thou hast redeemed the world.

From St. Thérèse

"My love discovers the charms of Your Face adorned with tears. I smile through my own tears when I contemplate Your sorrows.... Your beauty, which You know how to veil, discloses for me all its mystery.... Leave in me the Divine impress of Your Features filled with sweetness."

"Be another Veronica who wipes away the blood and tears of Jesus, her only Beloved."

"O Adorable Face of Jesus, the only Beauty that captivates my heart, deign to imprint in me Your Divine Likeness so that You may not behold the soul of Your little bride without seeing Yourself in her."

Glory Be ...

VII

JESUS FALLS THE SECOND TIME

"I was pushed hard, so that I was falling, but the Lord helped me." (Ps 118:13)

We adore Thee, O Christ, and we bless Thee,
Because by Thy Holy Cross, Thou hast redeemed the world.

From St. Thérèse

"Would you want to refuse to fall a hundred times, if that were necessary to prove your love for Him, rising each time with greater strength than before your fall?"

"To be little is not to become discouraged over one's faults, for children fall often, but they are too little to hurt themselves much."

"I will have the right of doing stupid things up until my death, if I am humble and if I remain little. Look at little children: they never stop breaking things, tearing things, falling down. When I fall in this way, it makes me realize my nothingness more."

Our Father...

VIII

JESUS MEETS THE WOMEN OF JERUSALEM

"And there followed Him a great multitude, including many women who mourned and lamented Him." (Lk 23:27)

We adore Thee, O Christ, and we bless Thee,
Because by Thy Holy Cross, Thou hast redeemed the world.

From St. Thérèse

"Jesus bears our imperfections patiently; He does not like teaching us everything at once, but normally enlightens us a little at a time."

"Every moment He is guiding and inspiring me. Most often it is not at prayer, but while I go about my day."

"Women, how they are misunderstood! And yet … during the Passion of Our Lord, women had more courage than the Apostles since they braved the insults of the soldiers and dared to dry the adorable Face of Jesus. It is undoubtedly because of this that He allows misunderstanding to be their lot on earth, since He chose it for Himself."

Hail Mary…

IX

JESUS FALLS A THIRD TIME

"He raises the poor from the dust, and lifts the needy from the ash heap." (Ps 113:7)

We adore Thee, O Christ, and we bless Thee,
Because by Thy Holy Cross, Thou hast redeemed the world.

From St. Thérèse

> "Why fear that you might not be able to carry that cross without growing weak? Didn't Jesus fall three times on His way to Calvary? And you, poor little child, should you not resemble your Bridegroom?"
>
> "To suffer our imperfections with patience is true sanctity, the source of peace."
>
> "Yes, I'm like a tired and harassed traveler, who reaches the end of his journey and falls over. Yes, but I'll be falling into God's arms!"

Glory Be . . .

X

JESUS IS STRIPPED

"He was oppressed, and He was afflicted, yet He opened not His mouth; like a lamb that is led to the slaughter, and like a sheep that before its shearers is dumb, so He opened not His mouth." (Is 53:7)

We adore Thee, O Christ, and we bless Thee,
Because by Thy Holy Cross, Thou hast redeemed the world.

From St. Thérèse

"Whenever I find myself faced with the prospect of an attack by the enemy, I am most courageous; I turn my back on him, without so much as looking at him, and run to Jesus."

"In one instant Jesus accomplished what I had been unable to do for several years, having been content, on my part, with my good will, which had never been wanting."

"What pleases the good God in my little soul is to see me love my littleness and my poverty, it is seeing the blind trust that I have in His mercy."

Our Father...

XI

JESUS IS NAILED TO THE CROSS

"A pack of evildoers encircles me. They have pierced my hands and feet; I can count all my bones while they stare at me and gloat." (Ps 22:16-17)

We adore Thee, O Christ, and we bless Thee,
Because by Thy Holy Cross, Thou hast redeemed the world.

From St. Thérèse

"He puts Himself at our mercy. He does not want to accept anything from us unless we give it with a good heart. He stretches out His hand to us to receive a little love. He cries, 'I thirst.'"

"He alone disposes the events of our life of exile.... It is the hand of Jesus that guides everything."

"It had been the sight of His Blood flowing from one of these very Wounds that had given me my thirst for souls."

Hail Mary ...

XII

JESUS DIES FOR US

*"Father, into Thy hands
I commend my spirit."* (Lk 23:46)

We adore Thee, O Christ, and we bless Thee,
Because by Thy Holy Cross, Thou hast redeemed the world.

From St. Thérèse

"Jesus has for us a love so incomprehensible, so delicate, that He does not want to do anything without associating us with Him. He wants us to participate with Him in the work of saving souls."

"Look at His adorable Face. Look at His glazed and sunken eyes. Look at His wounds. Look Jesus in the Face. There you will see how He loves us."

"At the moment when He expired, Jesus gave to His Father the greatest proof of love that was possible."

Glory Be . . .

XIII

JESUS IS TAKEN DOWN FROM THE CROSS AND PLACED IN HIS MOTHER'S ARMS

"One of the soldiers pierced His side with a lance, and immediately there came out blood and water." (Jn 19:34)

We adore Thee, O Christ, and we bless Thee,
Because by Thy Holy Cross, Thou hast redeemed the world.

From St. Thérèse

> "The Blessed Virgin Mary held her dead Jesus on her knees, and He was disfigured and covered with blood! Ah, I don't know how she stood it!"
>
> "I felt entirely hidden under the Blessed Mother's veil."
>
> "You came to smile at me in the morning of my life; come and smile at me again, Mother, now that it is eventide."

Our Father . . .

XIV

JESUS IS LAID IN THE TOMB

"And Joseph wrapped Him in a linen cloth and laid Him in a rock hewn tomb." (Lk 23:53)

"But on the first day of the week, they came to the tomb.... But they did not find the body of the Lord Jesus." (Lk 24:1,3)

We adore Thee, O Christ, and we bless Thee,
Because by Thy Holy Cross, Thou hast redeemed the world.

From St. Thérèse

"Jesus has chosen to show me the only way which leads to the Divine Furnace of love; it is the way of childlike self-surrender, the way of a child who sleeps, afraid of nothing, in its father's arms."

"Coming into this land of exile, You willed to suffer and to die in order to draw souls to the bosom of the Eternal Fire of the Blessed Trinity. Ascending once again to the Inaccessible Light, henceforth Your abode, You remain still in this valley of tears hidden beneath the appearances of a white Host."

"How little we know of the goodness and merciful love of Jesus."

For the intentions of the Holy Father: Our Father, Hail Mary, Glory Be.

"All those who were there and who saw what took place said: 'Truly this was the Son of God.'" (Mt 27:54)

From St. Thérèse

"Your Face, O my sweet Savior, is the divine bouquet of myrrh I want to keep on my heart."

Prayer to the Holy Face
O Jesus, who, in Thy cruel Passion didst become the "reproach of men and the Man of Sorrows," I worship Thy divine Face. Once it shone with the beauty and sweetness of the Divinity; but now, for my sake, it is become as "the face of a leper." Yet, in that disfigured Countenance, I recognize Thy infinite love, and I am consumed with the desire of making Thee loved by all mankind. The tears that flowed so abundantly from Thy Eyes are to me as precious pearls that I delight to gather, that with their worth I may ransom the souls of poor sinners. O Jesus, whose Face is the sole beauty that ravishes my heart, I may not see here below the sweetness of Thy glance, nor feel the ineffable tenderness of Thy kiss. I bow to Thy Will—but I pray Thee to imprint in me Thy divine likeness, and I implore Thee so to inflame me with Thy love, that it may quickly consume me, and that I may soon reach the vision of Thy glorious Face in heaven. Amen.

"Surely He has borne our griefs and carried our sorrows." (Is 53:4)

Prayer before a Crucifix

Look down upon me, good and gentle Jesus, while before Thy face I humbly kneel, and with burning soul I pray and beseech Thee to fix deep in my heart lively sentiments of faith, hope, and charity, true contrition for my sins, and a firm purpose of amendment; while I contemplate with great love and tender pity Thy five wounds, pondering over them within me, having in mind the words which David Thy prophet said of Thee, my Jesus: "They have pierced my hands and my feet; they have numbered all my bones."

For the intentions of the Holy Father: Our Father, Hail Mary, Glory Be.

A plenary indulgence is granted on any of the Fridays of Lent to the faithful who, after Communion, devoutly recite the above prayer before a crucifix.

Act of Oblation to Merciful Love

"Draw me, we will run." (Song of Songs 1:4)

✣

J.M.J.T.

Offering of Myself as a Victim of Holocaust to the Merciful Love of the Good God

O my God! Most Blessed Trinity, I desire to *Love* You and make You *Loved*, to work for the glory of Holy Church by saving souls on earth and liberating those suffering in purgatory. I desire to accomplish Your will perfectly and to reach the degree of glory You have prepared for me in Your Kingdom. I desire, in a word, to be a Saint, but I feel my helplessness and I beg You, O my God! to be Yourself my *Sanctity*!

Since You loved me so much as to give me Your only Son as my Savior and my Spouse, the infinite treasures of His merits are mine. I offer them to You with gladness, begging You to look upon me only in the Face of Jesus and in His Heart burning with *Love*.

I offer You, too, all the merits of the Saints (in Heaven and on earth), their acts of *Love*, and those of the Holy Angels. Finally, I offer You, *O Blessed Trinity!* the *Love* and merits of the *Blessed Virgin, my dear Mother*. It is to her I abandon my offering, begging her to present it to You.

Her Divine Son, my *Beloved* Spouse, told us in the days of His mortal life: *"Whatsoever you ask the Father in My name He will give it to you!"* I am certain, then, that You will grant my desires; I know, O my God! that *the more You want to give, the more You make us desire*. I feel in my heart immense desires and it is with confidence I ask You to come and take possession of my soul. Ah! I cannot receive Holy Communion as often as I desire, but, Lord, are You not *All-Powerful?* Remain in me as in a tabernacle and never separate Yourself from Your little victim.

I want to console You for the ingratitude of the wicked, and I beg of You to take away my freedom to displease You. If through weakness I sometimes fall, may Your *Divine Glance* cleanse my soul immediately, consuming all my imperfections like the fire that transforms everything into itself.

I thank You, O my God! for all the graces You have granted me, especially the grace of making me pass through the crucible of suffering. It is with joy I shall contemplate You on the Last Day carrying the scepter of Your Cross. Since You deigned to give me a share in this very precious Cross, I hope in Heaven to resemble You and to see shining in my glorified body the sacred stigmata of Your Passion.

After earth's Exile, I hope to go and enjoy You in the Fatherland, but I do not want to lay up merits for Heaven. I want to work for Your *Love alone* with the one purpose of pleasing You, consoling Your Sacred Heart, and saving souls who will love You eternally.

In the evening of this life, I shall appear before You with empty hands, for I do not ask You, Lord, to count my works. All our justice is stained in

Your eyes. I wish, then, to be clothed in your own *Justice* and to receive from Your *Love* the eternal possession of *Yourself*. I want no other *Throne*, no other *Crown* but *You*, my *Beloved!*

Time is nothing in Your eyes, and a single day is like a thousand years. You can, then, in one instant prepare me to appear before You.

In order to live in one single act of perfect Love, I OFFER MYSELF AS A VICTIM OF HOLOCAUST TO YOUR MERCIFUL LOVE, asking You to consume me incessantly, allowing the waves of *infinite tenderness* shut up within You to overflow into my soul, and that thus I may become a *Martyr* of Your *Love*, O my God!

May this martyrdom, after having prepared me to appear before You, finally cause me to die and may my soul take its flight without any delay into the eternal embrace of *Your Merciful Love*.

I want, O my *Beloved*, at each beat of my heart to renew this offering to You an infinite number of times, until the shadows having disappeared I may be able to tell You of my *Love* in an *Eternal Face to Face!*

A Note on Indulgences

An indulgence is a share in the infinite merits Christ gained for us and allows the Church, His Bride, to distribute on His behalf. Indulgences are plenary when all temporal punishment is wiped away and partial when some temporal punishment is wiped away. Whether plenary or partial, an indulgence may be gained for oneself or offered for a soul in purgatory.

To gain a plenary indulgence, that is, the remission of *all* temporal punishment due to one's sins, one must perform the act required for the indulgence and fulfill three conditions: sacramental confession (within 20 days), Holy Communion (on the day of the act, if possible), and prayer for the Holy Father's intentions (an Our Father and Hail Mary or other prayers). One sacramental confession suffices for several plenary indulgences, but each plenary indulgence requires its own

Communion and prayer for the Holy Father's intentions.

The final requirement to gain a plenary indulgence is detachment from all sin, even venial sin. This does not require the feeling of complete aversion to all sin, but rather a detachment in the will. The Act of Contrition expresses this in the words: "I detest all my sins because of Thy just punishment *but most of all because they offend Thee my God who art all good and deserving of all my love.*" Confident in God's mercy, one can also simply pray, "Dear Holy Spirit, if I am not detached from all sin, please make me detached now, so that I may gain this plenary indulgence that my Mother, the Church, offers to me, Her child."

These are the conditions, but the main effort one makes to gain a plenary indulgence is the performance of a particular action. While many plenary indulgences (and their required actions) are attached to specific days of the year—for instance, the plenary indulgence one can gain from reciting the Prayer before a Crucifix (as found in this booklet) after Communion on Fridays in

Lent—there are four plenary indulgences that can be gained every day of the year, though only one per day.

These are: (1) recitation of the Rosary in a church or family, religious community or pious association; (2) adoration of the Blessed Sacrament for half an hour; (3) reading Holy Scripture for half an hour; (4) making the Stations of the Cross in a church.

As the Catechism teaches, the Church grants indulgences, which are a share in the treasury of the merits of Christ and the Saints, not only to remit punishment, but also to encourage us in works of devotion, penance, and charity. May the angels assist us!

A Note on Special Plenary Indulgences in the Time of Coronavirus

Decree of the Apostolic Penitentiary

The gift of special Indulgences is granted to the faithful suffering from COVID-19 disease, commonly known as Coronavirus, as well as to health care workers, family members and all those who in any capacity, including through prayer, care for them.

"Be joyful in hope, patient in affliction, faithful in prayer" (Rom 12: 12). The words written by Saint Paul to the Church of Rome resonate throughout the entire history of the Church and guide the judgment of the faithful in the face of all suffering, sickness and calamity.

The present moment in which the whole of humanity, threatened by an invisible and insidious disease, which for some time now has become part of all our lives, is marked day after day by anguished fears, new uncertainties and above all widespread physical and moral suffering.

The Church, following the example of her Divine Master, has always had the care of the sick at heart. As Saint John Paul II points out, the value of human suffering is twofold: "It is supernatural because it is rooted in the divine mystery of the Redemption of the world, and it is likewise deeply human, because in it the person discovers himself, his own humanity, his own dignity, his own mission" (*Apostolic Letter Salvifici Doloris*, 31).

Pope Francis, too, in these recent days, has shown his paternal closeness and renewed his invitation to pray incessantly for those who are sick with the Coronavirus.

So that all those who suffer because of COVID-19, precisely in the mystery of this suffering, may rediscover "the same redemptive suffering of Christ" (ibid., 30), this Apostolic Penitentiary, *ex auctoritate Summi Pontificis*, trusting in the word of Christ the Lord and considering with a spirit of faith the epidemic currently underway, to be lived in a spirit of personal conversion, grants the gift of Indulgences in accordance with the following disposition.

The *Plenary Indulgence* is granted to the faithful suffering from Coronavirus, who are subject to quarantine by order of the health authority in hospitals or in their own homes if, with a spirit detached from any sin, they unite spiritually through the media to the celebration of Holy Mass, the recitation of the Holy Rosary, to the pious practice of the Way of the Cross or other forms of devotion, or if at least they will recite the Creed, the Lord's Prayer and a pious invocation to the Blessed Virgin Mary, offering this trial in a spirit of faith in God and charity towards their brothers and sisters, with the will to fulfil the usual conditions (sacramental confession, Eucharistic communion and prayer according to the Holy Father's intentions), as soon as possible.

Health care workers, family members and all those who, following the example of the Good Samaritan, exposing themselves to the risk of contagion, care for the sick of Coronavirus according to the words of the divine Redeemer: "Greater love has no one than this: to lay down one's life for one's friends" (Jn 15: 13), will obtain the same gift of the *Plenary Indulgence* under the same conditions.

This Apostolic Penitentiary also willingly grants a *Plenary Indulgence* under the same conditions on the occasion of the current world epidemic, also to those faithful who offer a visit to the Blessed Sacrament, or Eucharistic adoration, or reading the Holy Scriptures for at least half an hour, or the recitation of the Holy Rosary, or the pious exercise of the Way of the Cross, or the recitation of the Chaplet of Divine Mercy, to implore from Almighty God the end of the epidemic, relief for those who are afflicted and eternal salvation for those whom the Lord has called to Himself.

The Church prays for those who find themselves unable to receive the Sacrament of the Anointing of the Sick and of the Viaticum, entrusting each and every one to divine Mercy by virtue of the communion of saints and granting the faithful a *Plenary Indulgence* on the point of death, provided that they are duly disposed and have recited a few prayers during their lifetime (in this case the Church makes up for the three usual conditions required). For the attainment of this indulgence the use of the crucifix or the cross is recommended (cf. *Enchiridion indulgentiarum*, no.12).

May the Blessed Virgin Mary, Mother of God and of the Church, Health of the Sick and Help of Christians, our Advocate, help suffering humanity, saving us from the evil of this pandemic and obtaining for us every good necessary for our salvation and sanctification.

The present Decree is valid notwithstanding any provision to the contrary.

Given in Rome, from the seat of the Apostolic Penitentiary, on 19 March 2020.

Mauro Cardinal Piacenza
Major Penitentiary
Krzysztof Nykiel

Guardian Angel Prayer
(When Unable to Assist at Holy Mass)

Dear Guardian Angel, go for me to the church, there kneel down at Mass for me. At the Offertory, take me to God, and offer Him my service: What I am, what I have, offer as my gift. At the Consecration, with your seraphic strength, adore my Saviour truly present, praying for those who have loved me, for those who have offended me, and for those now deceased, that the blood of Jesus may purify them all. During Holy Communion, bring to me the Body and Blood of Jesus uniting Him with me in spirit, so that my heart may become His dwelling place. Plead with Him, that through His sacrifice all people throughout the world may be saved. When the Mass ends, bring home to me and to every home, the Lord's blessing. Amen.

"A few days after my Oblation to God's Merciful Love, I had commenced in the choir the Way of the Cross, when I felt myself suddenly wounded by a dart of fire so ardent that I thought I should die. I know not how to describe that transport; there is no comparison which would make the vehemence of that flame understood. It seemed as though an invisible force plunged me wholly into fire. Oh, that fire! What sweetness! One minute, one second more, and my soul must have been set free..."

—St. Thérèse (*Story of a Soul*)

"Few are the souls to receive this divine wound: those chiefly whose spirit and power are to be transmitted to their spiritual children: God bestows on the Founder such gifts and graces as shall be proportionate to the succession of the Order as the first-fruits of the Spirit."

—St. John of the Cross (*The Living Flame of Love*)

Inquiries about discount pricing for
bulk orders of print copies of this book
may be addressed to the publisher at:
littlewaybooks@gmail.com

www.ingramcontent.com/pod-product-compliance
Lightning Source LLC
Chambersburg PA
CBHW032359100526
44587CB00010BA/632